IMAGES
of America

EUREKA SPRINGS

ARKANSAS

This group of young people might be a theater company, traveling through the country and pausing to entertain the citizens of Eureka Springs. (Eureka Springs Historical Museum.)

IMAGES
of America

EUREKA SPRINGS

ARKANSAS

Kay Marnon Danielson

ARCADIA
PUBLISHING

Published by Arcadia Publishing
Charleston, South Carolina

Library of Congress Catalog Card Number: 2001094345

For all general information contact Arcadia Publishing at:
Telephone 843-853-2070
Fax 843-853-0044
E-Mail sales@arcadiapublishing.com
For customer service and orders:
Toll-Free 1-888-313-2665

Visit us on the Internet at www.arcadiapublishing.com

This nattily dressed young man sports a three-piece suit, a fine hat, and buckles on his shoes. (Bank of Eureka Springs.)

CONTENTS

ACKNOWLEDGMENTS

This publication would not have been possible without the diligent people who collect, preserve, garner, snip, and stow bits and pieces of history to save for future generations. My thanks go to Randy Wolfinbarger for his trust in lending his postcard collection to a stranger. My gratitude goes to John F. Cross of the Bank of Eureka Springs and Gladys Sands of the Eureka Springs Historical Museum who generously shared their fine historic photographic collections. The citizens of Eureka Springs offered hospitality and genuine old-time mountain-folk warmth that made the modern day work of creating a book a real pleasure.

INTRODUCTION

The land that became Arkansas was part of the 1803 Louisiana Purchase and white settlers started populating the area known as the Ozarks in the early 1820s for the free land and bountiful hunting it offered. While much of the land was forested, with rocky outcrops, settlers were able to grow enough produce and livestock to support growing families. In 1836, Arkansas was admitted to the Union as the 25th state.

The Civil War stung the area, taking men from their families and pitching a heated battle at nearby Pea Ridge. But it was in the years following the war that word of the healing properties of the bubbling springs in the Ozarks began to leak out. By the later part of the century, people were undertaking the arduous journey on foot or horseback to find relief from among other things, rheumatism, cancer, sore eyes, kidney disease, liver complaints, paralysis, ulcers, asthma, and the impure condition of the blood.

Eventually, trails made wagon and stagecoach travel possible, but it was the train that opened the area to tourism in 1883 with the first 18-mile spur from Missouri. The town prospered and made way for automobiles in the 1920s and even small airplanes carried visitors to Eureka Springs in the 1930s. But the days of thousands of visitors were numbered and the area fell into decline when post-World War II advances in medicine dimmed demand for healing waters. New roads and disposable income revived the tourist industry beginning in the 1960s and Eureka Springs has enjoyed growing popularity since then.

The photographs in this book reflect the story of the early days of settlement and the glorious boom times of Eureka Springs between the late 1800s to 1950s. Now it is one of a dozen towns designated as a "Distinctive Destination" by the National Trust for Historic Preservation.

These two young women with starched white skirts and tiny waistlines sat for their photograph around the turn of the century. (Author's collection.)

Most of the early photographic images were either studio portraits or outdoor scenes. Those occasional ones taken indoors tell a lot about how people lived. This unidentified woman appears to have the picture of the two young women shown above displayed on her dresser. (Author's collection.)

One

EARLY TIMES

In the early 1800s, pioneers from Tennessee and Kentucky came to the Ozarks seeking a new beginning, having left behind what they considered "too crowded" conditions. They found the new land challenging with rugged inclines and a rocky landscape. But there was also bountiful game, a mild climate, and, of course, healing waters.

Johnson and Oil Springs are only 2 of the 63 springs eventually found in the area. (Randy Wolfinbarger.)

The Natural Falls is one of the many serene spots that nature created with wind, rock, and water for man to enjoy. (Randy Wolfinbarger.)

The beauty of Immersion Pool drew visitors like these men in 1909. (Randy Wolfinbarger.)

Pivot Rock, a natural formation of wind eroded stone, drew sightseers from the early times. (Eureka Springs Historical Museum.)

Many early settlers found refuge in caves and lived in them for some time. L.J. Kalklosch wrote in *The Healing Fountain* (Eureka Springs, Ark., 1881) that "the entrances being very large are closed with boards, making very comfortable dwelling places. One has seven rooms and is used as a boarding house. Some of the rooms have rock floors, rock walls and rock top. This writer engaged one of these romantic rooms in which to finish this work." (Bank of Eureka Springs.)

Water gushed from the massive rocks and lush forests in the Ozarks. Mystic Spring was a popular stop for tourists. (Bank of Eureka Springs.)

Even in the early years of settlement, women managed to keep up with the fashions that included hair bows and gold lockets or watches. (Author's collection.)

This scene from the White River area gives rise to the imagination when wondering how the pioneers ever made it into the Ozarks and how they managed to eventually build the railroad in 1883. (Randy Wolfinbarger.)

Early settlement of the area required teams of animals for heavy work. Sometimes the animals provided a chance for a photograph to send to family far away. (Author's collection.)

Early settlers cut their own timber but soon sawmill operations fed the need for building materials in the growing community. (Eureka Springs Historical Museum.)

Eventually the raised shacks gave way to better designed houses and buildings. Many, like the small bungalow here, survive and are now in service as private dwellings or Bed and Breakfast inns. (Author's collection.)

Two

TRANSPORTATION

Getting to the healing waters took some doing. Up until the late 1800s, travel to this area was on foot or horseback. When rough trails were blazed, horse, mule, and oxen-drawn wagons made the journey carrying families and their belongings. When stagecoach lines connected the 85 miles between Ozark, Arkansas, and Eureka Springs, it was a 24-hour journey. Pierce City, Missouri, was a mere 45 miles and 9 hours in the lurching coach. When the trains began operation in 1883, it was estimated that 125 people a day came to Eureka Springs.

The livery services provided an animal or carriage for rent. When the hotels opened, horseback riding was offered as one of the entertainments and the liveries provided the animals and guides. (Bank of Eureka Springs.)

Carriages and wagons were the conveyance of the day. They were used for pleasure rides as well as carrying goods and transport. (Eureka Springs Historical Museum.)

This father took his children for a ride in their horse and buggy. (Bank of Eureka Springs.)

Oxen teams were often the preferred stock. While they only traveled about two miles an hour, they were steady and would pull tremendous loads. (Eureka Springs Historical Museum.)

While transportation improved with the decades so did mail service. This unusual studio portrait shows a women reading a letter. (Author's collection.)

When a family had to move, everything was stowed in the wagon and then off they went. (Eureka Springs Historical Museum.)

Even in the early days, the healing water was taken from the springs and hauled by wagon to supply people who couldn't get to the source. (Bank of Eureka Springs.)

The coming of the train opened Eureka Springs to a flood of visitors in the late 1800s. (Randy Wolfinbarger.)

Several trains a day rode the rails to Eureka Springs. This crew was with the St. Louis and North Arkansas Railroad. (Bank of Eureka Springs.)

White River Bridge, near Eureka Springs, Ark.

Before the trains could come, many bridges had to be built. This one once spanned the White River. (Randy Wolfinbarger.)

Where there are trains, sometimes there are wrecks. (Bank of Eureka Springs.)

M. & N. A. Ry. Station. Eureka Springs, Ark.

About 1930, the train depot was a busy place with cars and trolleys waiting for passengers from the next arrival. (Randy Wolfinbarger.)

A capitalist from St. Louis, Mr. Kerens—third from the left on the steps—built the Kerens Chapel and generously supported St. Elizabeth Church. He owned his own private rail car, the *Frisco*, shown here. (Eureka Springs Historical Museum.)

Not only did the train have to ford rivers, it had to go through mountains. It was a big day in 1883 when the first train came through the Narrows, a passageway cut through the mountain. (Bank of Eureka Springs.)

Trolley cars provided local transportation and entertainment. Horses or mules pulled early ones. (Randy Wolfinbarger.)

The trolleys were set up to pass by many of the hotels as well as the most popular springs. This one makes a stop at Grotto Springs. (Randy Wolfinbarger.)

One of the medium-sized accommodations, the Waverly House Hotel was popular for its moderate rates. (Bank of Eureka Springs.)

MAGNETIC SPRINGS HOTEL Rooms, Large, Light and Airy. BATHS IN HOUSE

ALL HEALTH FOODS PROVIDED AT REGULAR RATES

Convenient to Springs. Write for Particulars

CHAUTAUQUA HOUSE,

J. S. VINCENT, Proprietor.

Pleasantly located on Spring Street, on Street Car Line.

THE WAVERLY.

MRS. M. E. GUFFY, Prop.

..ly furnished. On Car line, near Post Office. Convenient to the principal springs. Every room o..tside, cool and light, affording a beautiful view of the city and country.

Rate per day $1.50, per week $6.00 to $7.00

THACH COTTAGE

J. T. WADDILL, Proprietor.

Located on Mountain and on Street Car Line.

GRAND CENTRAL HOTEL.

R. M. THORNTON, Proprietor.

Newly Fitted and furnished. The only Brick Fire-proof Hotel in the City. A Sample Room for Salesmen in Connection. Onyx Spring Water on each floor. Rates, $1 a day; $4 to $6 a week.

MAIN STREET.

BISHOP'S BAZAAR

FINE CANDIES AND SOUVENIRS

OUR SPECIALTIES

BISHOP BLOCK SPRING ST.

First-Class in Every Respect

PENCE HOUSE,

J. W. PENCE, Prop.

Good Sample Room for Commercial Men.

Located on North Spring Street on Electric Car Line.

Office Phone 24, Res. Phone 10.

DR. R. G. FLOYD,

RESIDENT PHYSICIAN.

Hours, 9 a. m, to 12 m., 1:30 to 4:30 p. m.

Telephone No. 80, Goods Delivered

CONGRESS SPRING GROCERY

G. H. McLAUGHLIN, Proprietor

A modern, fully up-to-date house, where you will always find a complete line of Staple and Fancy Edibles.

M. R. REGAN, M. D.

HOMEOPATHIST.

Catarrhal Disorders, Chronic Diseases.

Phones, Office 32, Residence 37.

PELL & DIDDEA,

Leading Jewelers and Opticians.......

Repairing Neatly Done. Duncan Block.

M. F. GEAR,

EUREKA WATER SHIPPER,

Water from any of the springs shipped on short notice . . . .

The Only Carbonating Plant in the City.

PORCH & CROOK

The Leading Druggists.

WADSWORTH-FLOYD BLOCK

Opposite Postoffice.

Service UP TO DATE For Particulars Address Magnetic Springs Hotel Dr. C. A. Reed, Prop.

LEADING HOTELS AND BUSINESS FIRMS

Many visitors had only the local hotel ads to determine where to stay and they had a lot to choose from. (Bank of Eureka Springs.)

When everyone started buying automobiles and roads became necessary, convict labor was used to construct the roads through the mountains. In a time before heavy road equipment, it required drilling and blasting the rock and hard labor to remove it all. The highways were not paved until after World War II. (Bank of Eureka Springs.)

The convict tent quarters housed the men and provided weekend entertainment when the convicts put on a show for the civilians. (Bank of Eureka Springs.)

The White River was first spanned for the train, but in the 1920s the increasingly popular automobile required their own bridges. (Bank of Eureka Springs.)

By the late 1920s, even middle-class families could afford a car and travel became more common. This family stopped at Harding Spring in their Model T. (Bank of Eureka Springs.)

The roads followed the natural contours of the mountaintops and often ended up serpentine and curvy. (Randy Wolfinbarger.)

Some of the sightseeing conveyances were more utilitarian than comfortable. (Eureka Springs Historical Museum.)

This truckload of people was on a sightseeing trip. (Eureka Springs Historical Museum.)

Dr. Albert Tatman takes a pleasure drive with members of his family. (Eureka Springs Historical Museum.)

Three

VISITORS

Many of the photographs in the Eureka Springs archives are unidentified. Unquestionably many of these faces are those of visitors, as thousands came from all over the country. Some stayed for a few days or a week but others stayed for months. Their images and part of their lives contributed to the story of the place.

A picture at one of the springs was a must for most of the visitors to Eureka Springs. These women visited around the turn of the century. (Eureka Springs Historical Museum.)

Art Study from   *The Sketch Book*

Pose by Miss Jennie Foy, the Beautiful and Popular Sister of Mr.
Mike Foy, of Musical Fame Among Arkansaw Travelers.

The Sketch Book claims to be the handsomest publication in the south and makes good at sight. It will celebrate its first birthday with the next issue and its mamma invites all persons interested in orphan babies to send it a dollar subscription for a birthday present. Every little bit will help provide nourishment for this growing baby magazine during its hard second year when it must cut teeth and learn to walk. ✻ ✻ ✻ ✻ ✻ ✻ ✻ ✻ ✻ ✻ Now is the time.

ARKANSAW TRAVELERS
NUMBER

The midsummer issue will be featured especially for travelling men. It will contain a special drawing on insert mount, "Arkansaw Traveler's Girl;" cartoon picturing organization of the Travelers together with the cabin, razorback, hound, rooster and the boys; "The Drummer's Summer Girl"—good enough to eat; storiettes for the man with the grip, and portraits of leading traveling men. The Arkansaw Traveler who does not have this issue will lay himself liable to the charge of traveling "on a slow freight through Arkansaw." Make connection with the subscription list of the Sketch Book. It's the proper thing to do. The tax is only one dollar per annum.

SKETCH BOOK QUARTERLY,
LITTLE ROCK, ARK.

The Arkansas Travelers published the *Sketch Book Quarterly* for their members. (Eureka Springs Historical Museum.)

The Arkansas Travelers was a group of businessmen who traveled all over the state, visiting different areas. (Bank of Eureka Springs.)

This image leaves it to our imagination to figure out why there are 16 young men and only 1 bicycle. (Bank of Eureka Springs.)

The "Talleyho" was a large carriage or coach drawn by six or eight horses for large sightseeing groups. This group of children was enjoying a tour of the town. (Bank of Eureka Springs.)

These 39 young girls celebrated State's Day that included Arizona—the 48th state admitted to the Union. There is no record of why the other nine states were omitted. (Bank of Eureka Springs)

Four

THE TOWN

It is hard to imagine the current Eureka Springs with a population of less than 2,000 as a boomtown, but in 1880 it was estimated that 15,000 people were in the area. The weather, advances in transportation and medicine, and the economic health of the country as a whole, influenced frequent fluctuation in population.

This scene of Eureka Springs was taken from Magnetic Mountain around the turn of the century. (Bank of Eureka Springs.)

Spring Street retains many of the buildings that were there 100 years ago but now the streets are paved and automobiles have replaced the trolley tracks. It is reported that none of the 250 streets in Eureka Springs cross at right angles. (Randy Wolfinbarger.)

There are few level spots in the mountains and houses often cling to hillsides. This sometimes required building bridges over the gullies. These enterprising folks found an unusual opportunity for a photograph. (Eureka Springs Historical Museum.)

The distinctive roof of the City Hall building eventually succumbed to the ravages of time and was replaced. In 2001, the roof required repairs and at this time the city took great pains to replicate the original design as closely as possible. (Randy Wolfinbarger.)

The Commercial Club Band was made up of businessmen who played for special occasions. It was the forerunner of the Chamber of Commerce organization. (Eureka Springs Historical Museum.)

Many of the turn-of-the-century homes remain in Eureka Springs and now serve as bed and breakfast inns. Fortunately, the streets have now been paved. (Bank of Eureka Springs.)

This 1918 view of the Carnegie Library and St. Elizabeth's Catholic Church illustrates some of the fine stonework found in Eureka Springs. Both buildings are still in use. (Randy Wolfinbarger.)

Horseback riding was one of the most popular activities for hotel guests and the larger establishments had their own stables. These local young men worked for the livery stable and guided groups of horseback riders on the trails. (Eureka Springs Historical Museum.)

While it only snowed periodically, it is not an unknown form of precipitation in Arkansas. These ladies enjoyed the novelty around 1890. (Randy Wolfinbarger.)

Howell Avenue was similar to many other streets in the village—with houses appearing to be stacked on top of one another. (Randy Wolfinbarger.)

There were many photographers in the town that hosted thousands of visitors but Gray's Studio was one of the most active. Pictures were posted on the porch columns and sold for 10¢ each with pictures printed for 5¢ each. (Bank of Eureka Springs.)

While no known pictures of the photographer Lucian Gray have survived, his son appeared in some of his father's work. (Randy Wolfinbarger.)

Little Photographer Gray, Youngest Opossum Hunter in Eureka Springs, Ark.

Gray's ad appeared with some of the other local businesses. One can only guess how a Kodak could be rented free. (Bank of Eureka Springs.)

40

View from South Mountain,
Eureka Springs, Ark.

Most of the panoramic scenes taken of Eureka Springs after 1886 showcase the Crescent Hotel, the town's crown jewel, that sat atop the mountain and was visible for miles. Built at a cost over $250,000 it was 5-stories high and built of local stone, lit with gas, and heated with steam. (Randy Wolfinbarger.)

MEAT MARKET.

The Schnitizer and McLaughlin Meat Market served the town at 188 Spring Street and is pictured in this 1912 scene. (Bank of Eureka Springs.)

Originally Eureka Springs was filled with shacks thrown up to house the thousands of people who rushed to the area after 1880. But soon people wanted substantial, moderately-priced housing and W.O. Perkins (in the window dressed in coat) supplied many of them. (Bank of Eureka Springs.)

W.O. Perkins photographed most of the houses he built and left that historic record for future generations to appreciate. (Bank of Eureka Springs.)

Construction on the Municipal Auditorium in downtown Eureka Springs began in 1928. (Eureka Springs Historical Museum.)

The Municipal Auditorium stands today and is still serving the community. (Randy Wolfinbarger.)

43

The Post Office was dedicated in 1917 and remains today, but other buildings now surround it. (Bank of Eureka Springs.)

For many years, the mule-powered trolleys transported people around the city, sometimes even entertaining passengers with a band. (Bank of Eureka Springs.)

Sitting on Basin Park, the Southern Hotel offered reasonable prices and a great view—until it burned to the ground. (Eureka Springs Historical Museum.)

Outdoor sales always draw a crowd and this one in the 1920s was no exception. (Bank of Eureka Springs.)

Eureka Springs' law enforcement officers were recorded on film. G.C. Pike, the chief of police, is shown on the right. (Bank of Eureka Springs.)

The First National Bank robbery was famous in the annals of Eureka Springs' history. On September 27, 1922, five men attempted to rob the bank but a foot alarm alerted citizens and a shootout commenced. Three of the men died and the two survivors went to prison. Many photographs were taken of the heroes. (Bank of Eureka Springs.)

The getaway driver was shot and the car rolled into a telephone pole while the robbery was taking place. The numbers of rescuers grew as news of the attempted heist spread. (Bank of Eureka Springs.)

Fire was a constant danger, especially in the wooden structures built around the turn of the century. This house belonged to Police Chief Pike. (Bank of Eureka Springs.)

Firefighters were an important part of the community, particularly with Eureka Springs' history. Four major fires occurred between 1883 and 1893, but even after that, sporadic loss of property and life occurred. (Eureka Springs Historical Museum.)

From the very earliest times of settlement, churches have been part of the landscape. By 1881, Catholic, Methodist, Baptist, Presbyterian, and Christian groups were listed as part of the business directory. The Christian Church building is shown in the 1930s. (Eureka Springs Historical Museum.)

Technology was welcomed in the mountains, and in 1898 J.W. Hill introduced the first telephone exchange. (Bank of Eureka Springs.)

The telephone exchange was housed in Hill's Transfer and Livery office. (Bank of Eureka Springs.)

Site of the original healing spring, Basin Park became the focal center of the town and remains as a site for public entertainment and a meeting place. (Eureka Springs Historical Museum.)

This group of young men is part of the Preparedness Company military unit. (Eureka Springs Historical Museum.)

The Thatch Cottage had a humble beginning, in 1880, as a four-room house. It eventually grew to 100 rooms and was a highly respected hotel until a fire destroyed it in a few hours in March of 1932. (Randy Wolfinbarger.)

Magnetic Spring is celebrated in the post card with a man reported to be 100 years of age—talk about subtle advertising. (Randy Wolfinbarger.)

This crew of men and animals were among the many who worked on the WPA project at Lake Leatherwood. They came from all around the country, assigned to work during the Depression on community projects. (Eureka Springs Historical Museum.)

Building a water supply for the community meant a reliable supply. This was the groundwork for the Bass Lake reservoir. (Bank of Eureka Springs.)

Seen here nearing completion, the dam at Lake Leatherwood was built as a flood control measure and was an example of the fine stonework found in the area. (Bank of Eureka Springs.)

Lake Leatherwood is 85 acres in size, one-and-a-quarter-miles long and has three miles of shoreline. It is now a city park. (Randy Wolfinbarger.)

Lake Leatherwood provided citizens with recreational camping, boating, fishing, and swimming. (Randy Wolfinbarger.)

Local historian Cora Pinkley-Call had this photograph made for her book, *Stair-Step-Town*, to illustrate the up-and-down of Eureka Springs. (Eureka Springs Historical Museum.)

Five

BUSINESS

The commerce of Eureka Springs began with health. But as soon as people gathered, there was a need for the basics of life, including sawmills, boarding houses, groceries, and every other thing to accommodate the living standard of the time. These are some of the business interests found in Eureka Springs. (Randy Wolfinbarger.)

The Baker Hospital was founded by Norman Baker, a physician from the Midwest who bought the Crescent and set up practice in Eureka Springs. Baker was one of many—dozens of doctors came to the area, some of which were more reputable then others. (Randy Wolfinbarger.)

The early hotels required laundry services, and these women worked hard to fill the need for clean sheets and clothing for guests. (Eureka Springs Historical Museum.)

The driver of the Eureka Springs Steam Laundry, "Fine Linens our Specialty"—delivered his work and impressed the ladies. (Eureka Springs Historical Museum.)

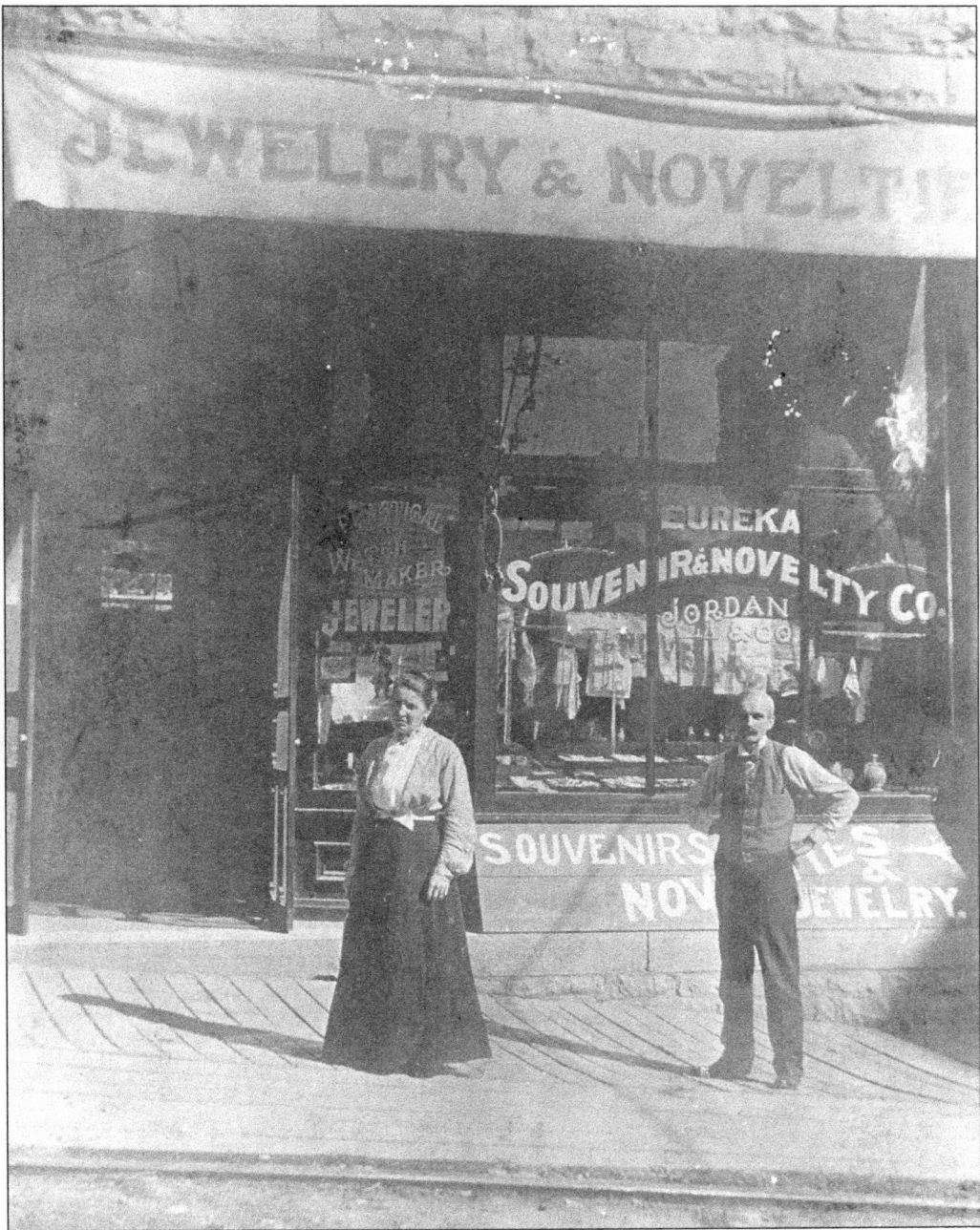

Some businesses have not changed much in 120 years. This store offered jewelry, souvenirs, and novelties—the same as many of the shops open today. (Eureka Springs Historical Museum.)

The First National Bank interior is pictured early in the century. Modern visitors can see what the old banks looked like by stepping into the lobby of the Bank of Eureka Springs on South Main Street. The entirely up-to-date bank has gone to great lengths to recreate the old look, with vintage roll-top desks, a couple early safes, and lots of historic photographs on the wall. Stop in and take a look. (Bank of Eureka Springs.)

The ads of the day can tell something about a town. Here the bank, shoe, and drug stores entice customers to try them out. (Bank of Eureka Springs.)

Meat markets have changed dramatically since McLaughlin's hung animal carcasses at room temperature and selections were cut to order. (Bank of Eureka Springs.)

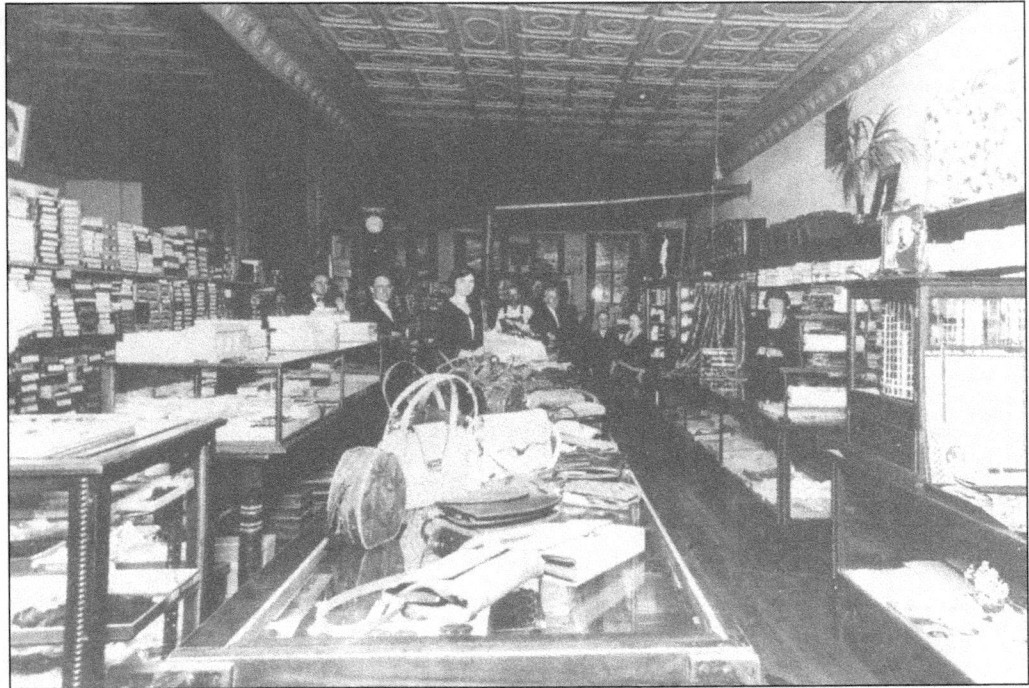

Around 1920, the Walker Brothers store offered most anything you could need or want. (Bank of Eureka Springs.)

Recycling was a way of life during the Depression; it was just called something different. This woman was a familiar sight as she collected discarded items and found uses for them. (Bank of Eureka Springs.)

Kappen's Market served the people of Eureka Springs around 1930. (Bank of Eureka Springs.)

It is lost to history just why these men were congregated at the Post Office and the *Daily Herald* Building, but what ever it was, it drew a crowd. (Bank of Eureka Springs.)

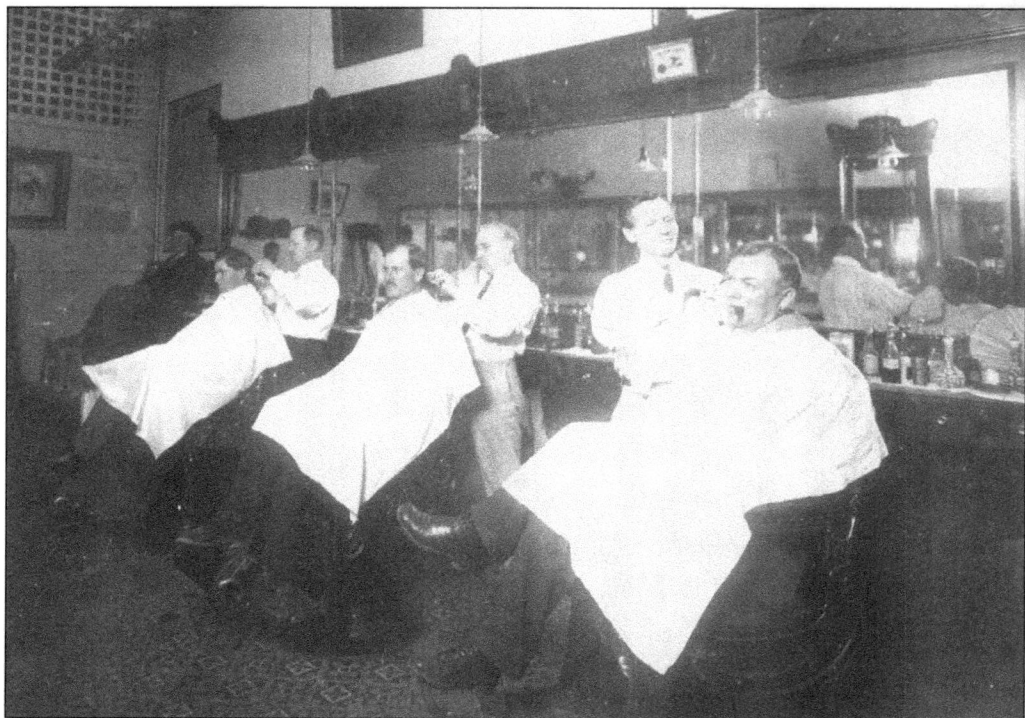

The barbershop was a place for men to gather, relax, and learn the latest news, while getting their hair trimmed. (Eureka Springs Historical Museum.)

Oil was never a big industry in the Ozarks, but that didn't stop the prospecting. The Sure Pop Oil Company started a drilling test in 1921 west of Eureka Springs, near the White River. (Eureka Springs Historical Museum.)

In October 1921, a barbecue for 2,100 people was held at the derrick—presumably some of these people were investors. Unfortunately, the Sure Pop well never hit oil and in July 1922, the well burned to the ground in a fire of unknown origin. (Bank of Eureka Springs.)

The McLaughlin Grocery on Spring Street was well-known for its artful display of goods and it was said a lady could go from the handsomest drawing room to McLaughlin's without offense to her aesthetic taste. (Bank of Eureka Springs.)

With so many physicians in Eureka Springs, doctors had to compete for business and most advertised in the popular press of the day. (Bank of Eureka Springs.)

THE WONDERS OF THE WATER THAT BUILT A CITY.

THE fact that the waters of Eureka Springs are the purest on earth, that their purity is such that when exposed to the sun for years in sealed bottles it still remains pure and odorless, losing none of its crystalline clearness, and when put through a cooling process seems to maintain all its original qualities in taste and purity, is one of the marvels that experiments have demonstrated. This experiment has been made over and over again, with recurring success. It establishes the fact that there are no impurities in the waters from these springs—that there is nothing in its composition to decompose. And this fact also explains the wonder and growing popularity of "Ozarka," the trade name given these waters by the Eureka Springs Water Company, who have builded a business that is a pride to the city, an advertisement of its health giving waters, and a protection as well. For in the absolute purity of the water they sell and ship, they realize their future business depends, and the investment that they have made must be protected by the maintenance of an untarnished reputation.

To maintain this every possible precaution has been taken. Their plant is equipped with all the essentials of modern machinery and sterilization. They use

THE "OZARKA" GIRL

nothing but glass containers and each of these is sealed at the springs, and their seal is an assurance of absolute purity. While they ship many carloads of water each month, every quart is contained in sealed glass vessels. To handle a business of this magnitude they have erected three beautiful stone buildings, and are contemplating further enlargements. They employ experienced men, who work under the strictest sanitary regulations. : : : : :

They have established agencies in all the principal cities of the great Southwest, some twenty in number, and in all of this great section "Ozarka" is becoming recognized as a household essential. It is the great table water that graces the board of those who recognize that pure water is a necessity in the maintenance of good health.

It is the boon to thousands of homes of the alkali plains, where it is impossible to get pure and palatable water through other sources.

The Eureka Springs Water Company is equipped by years of experience to market water with credit to the resort. "Ozarka" is their registered trade mark, and this label on a bottle is a guarantee against substitution. "Ozarka" upon the label means Eureka Springs Water, as pure as the water originally flows from its health giving springs. : : : : : : : :

This industry is the principal one in Eureka Springs. It furnishes to those who have not the means or time to come to Eureka Springs the pure, health-giving waters. To be sure, we cannot ship to you the ozone from our pine forests, our charming mountain scenery, or the air which aids in the rejuvenating process which has cured so many thousands of health seekers, but the next best thing to coming to Eureka Springs and drinking the health-giving waters, is to have the health-giving waters shipped to you. In addition to their water shipping business they have one of the finest carbonating plants in the United States, and are producing a high class of carbonated products. Their "Ozarka" Ginger Ale is gaining renown. The principal agencies of this company are located in St. Louis, Kansas City, Oklahoma City, Dallas, Fort Smith and Little Rock. : : : :

W. M. Duncan, President of the Citizens Bank, and identified with many of the principal interests of the resort, is the president of this company. Myron D. Jordan, Manager of the Citizens Electric Company, and one of the brilliant young business men of the Southwest, is the vice-president of the company. C. C. McCarty, one of the most jovial and popular of business hustlers, a man who is known all over the great Southwest, is business manager of the company, with headquarters in St. Louis. They are after your consideration, and if the delivering of purity in sealed bottles is any argument, then they are going to get it. And they will deliver the goods.

GET THE "OZARKA" HABIT.

Ozarka Water was one of the local products that had an eager market outside of the area. (Eureka Springs Historical Museum.)

Ozarka bottled water was served at many functions, such as this 1900 dinner. (Eureka Springs Historical Museum.)

Even the train station sported an Ozarka sign. (Eureka Springs Historical Museum.)

The Eureka Springs Water Company's Ozarka Water was shipped by the rail cars, so the bottled water went far and wide. (Eureka Springs Historical Museum.)

Spring water remained a big business, until the patent was purchased by Coca-Cola around 1943, and operations moved out of state. A Texas company bought the name and you can still buy the label Ozarka, but it no longer comes from Eureka Springs. (Eureka Springs Historical Museum.)

In the 1930s, motor travel became more affordable for a lot of Americans. Once again Eureka Springs became a destination and motor courts sprang up. Sam Leath, a horseback tour guide, started Camp Leath (later renamed Mount Air), which still has roots in the town today. (Randy Wolfinbarger.)

The interior of the Mount Air Motel advertised the restaurant's cooking. It was famous for Myrtie Mae's chicken dinners that she started cooking in her home in the 1920s. You can still find great chicken in the Myrtie Mae's tradition—now at the restaurant of the same name in the Inn of the Ozarks. (Randy Wolfinbarger.)

EUREKA COTTAGE CAMP
EUREKA SPRINGS, ARKANSAS
15 Cabins, 25 Rooms, $1.00 to $2.25
Games   ON 62 HIGHWAY   Shade

2089-P

Cottage motels sprang up during the 1930s, '40s and even '50s to fill demand for vacation lodgings. Today, many of these modernized cottages remain, retaining the flavor of a time past in Eureka Springs. (Randy Wolfinbarger.)

This 1958 postcard view of the Sky Line Motel is typical of the time. (Randy Wolfinbarger.)

71

Long known for quality mountain crafts, today Eureka Springs boasts a thriving artists' colony. (Eureka Springs Historical Museum.)

This 1954 grocery store interior marks a part of the past. (Bank of Eureka Springs.)

Sparkling in the sun, numerous rock shops still are found in the Ozarks. (Bank of Eureka Springs.)

Zoe Pike Harp—craftsperson, musician, and community leader—married into the Harp family that advertised their store as the oldest grocery in Eureka Springs. (Bank of Eureka Springs.)

This is a quiet street scene from the 1940s. (Bank of Eureka Springs.)

Six

SCHOOLS

While many of the existing photographs in the Eureka Springs vast collection are unidentified and could well be visitors from out of state, the school pictures are more easily claimed. The children photographed grew up in the area and represent the families that made the town what it is today.

These proud young graduates donned the boards and had their picture taken for the occasion around 1900. (Eureka Springs Historical Museum.)

The High School and Industrial Arts Building appear on this vintage postcard. (Randy Wolfinbarger.)

Boys will be boys and the two in the front row (to the left), have made their joke—standing pigeon toed for the group photograph. (Eureka Springs Historical Museum.)

This third-grade class was pictured in front of one of the local storefronts, a popular place for group shots. (Eureka Springs Historical Museum.)

The interior of a classroom about 1930 finds the children studying sentences and multiplication tables. A long paper chain decorates the corner of the room. (Eureka Springs Historical Museum.)

There are 40 children in this group. Apparently, large classrooms have been around for a long time. (Eureka Springs Historical Museum.)

These young men and women are ready to face the world after graduating high school in 1915. (Bank of Eureka Springs.)

Miss Crystal Davis' graduation was celebrated in her home with many flowers. (Eureka Springs Historical Museum.)

These children are pictured with books and baseball equipment. (Eureka Springs Historical Museum.)

I am looking for the letter that you owe m...

Crescent ~~Hotel~~ College Eureka Springs, Ark. *I am enjoying my College work very much...*

The Crescent Hotel served many purposes over the years—hotel, school, hospital, and spa. For several years it served as a women's college of nursing. (Randy Wolfinbarger.)

While some changes have taken place, the Crescent fireplace is unmistakable and is still an impressive sight to modern visitors. (Bank of Eureka Springs.)

The spacious lobby, with tall ceilings, still welcomes its guests and visitors. (Bank of Eureka Springs.)

Some of the Crescent College graduates pose for a picture on the train. (Bank of Eureka Springs.)

Women's basketball went back a long way. (Eureka Springs Historical Museum.)

This team pounded the courts in 1917. (Eureka Springs Historical Museum.)

Seven

PEOPLE

Mountain people were often characterized as being backwoods and known for their rough living, but there were a great variety of lifestyles in Eureka Springs. The following photographs include local people as well as visitors to the town. It is hard to tell the difference in many cases.

Some mountain folks eked out a living from the land and had few conveniences to show for it. (Eureka Springs Historical Museum.)

Elaborate fashions were often seen on the streets of Eureka Springs. This young woman's hat is decorated with feathers and bows. (Eureka Springs Historical Museum.)

This group of somber adults and a child may have been an extended family on holiday, around 1900. (Eureka Springs Historical Museum.)

Many photographs allow a glimpse of the family's surroundings and occasionally some notation gives clues to identities. (Eureka Springs Historical Museum.)

Members of the Jordan family were generous benefactors to the Eureka Springs Hospital. (Eureka Springs Historical Museum.)

Crystal Davis, daughter of Dr. Davis, is shown with a giant plant. The young woman was from a well-to-do family and her activities were often documented. (Eureka Springs Historical Museum.)

Crystal Davis' 1911 wedding to an attorney, Mr. Lyle of Michigan, was a celebrated affair. The couple moved to Michigan but within a decade, Crystal moved back to Eureka Springs with her daughter and lived in the Crystal Terrace until her death in the 1970s. (Eureka Springs Historical Museum.)

A publication of the time informed its readers that all the lovely young women shown in this photograph were married shortly after it was taken in 1907. (Eureka Springs Historical Museum.)

Is this a mother and daughter or a nanny with her charge? In either case it is a charming photo of a special time spent on the riverbank. (Eureka Springs Historical Museum.)

Identified as the Perkins girls, this trio gives a glimpse of a time long gone. (Eureka Springs Historical Museum.)

This group might be the staff of one of the larger hotels. (Eureka Springs Historical Museum.)

A father, with his boy and a dog, had this casual moment in their life put to film. (Eureka Springs Historical Museum.)

These intrepid travelers were part of a 1919 tourist club. (Eureka Springs Historical Museum.)

There were few black families living in Eureka Springs in the early part of the century but some prospered and did well. (Eureka Springs Historical Museum.)

Fashion dictated dress around the turn of the century, so women wore long skirts, fancy hats, and constricting clothes—even while exploring the mountain scenery. (Eureka Springs Historical Museum.)

Catherine Tina Hill was not a year old when she sat for her portrait in Eureka Springs. (Eureka Springs Historical Museum.)

Carrie Nation, famous for her war on drink, lived in Hatchet House for several years. The house remains and is open for guests as a museum. (Randy Wolfinbarger.)

Carrie A. Nation Enjoying a Drink of Eureka Springs Water, Eureka Springs, Ark.

Hiking and a picnic were favorites for all ages. A couple of the people carry a hiking stick—a popular local industry since the late 1800s. (Eureka Springs Historical Museum.)

McCollister,   Eureka Springs, Ark.

There have always been a lot of weddings in Eureka Springs and it is especially true today. Over 5,000 licenses are applied for annually, can be obtained quickly, and many places have walk-in ceremonies available. (Eureka Springs Historical Museum.)

Dr. James was rector of the St. James Episcopal Church in 1901. (Eureka Springs Historical Museum.)

Mother James helped her husband throughout his long career. (Eureka Springs Historical Museum.)

The Nave family is pictured around 1880. (Eureka Springs Historical Museum.)

Mr. Riley's horse spooked at the camera shutter but his young son managed to hold on. (Eureka Springs Historical Museum.)

Like many early settlers, this rural couple raised their family on the farm rather than choosing town life. (Eureka Springs Historical Museum.)

Many establishments offered childcare for parents who were enjoying the busy activities of Eureka Springs. (Eureka Springs Historical Museum.)

These young professional men look ready to make their mark in the world. (Eureka Springs Historical Museum.)

The Golfs family gathered in the late 1800s to have their picture made in a photographer's studio. Photography is still a big part of Eureka Springs' commerce and many visitors today step into a studio and have their visit recorded. (Eureka Springs Historical Museum.)

This young woman is unnamed, except as the girl with a braid. (Eureka Springs Historical Museum.)

Dr. Pearl Hale Tatman attended medical school, returned to Eureka Springs to practice, and married a fellow physician—Albert Tatman. She served her patients and the community for many years. (Eureka Springs Historical Museum.)

As in other wars, many young Arkansas men went to serve their country in World War I. (Eureka Springs Historical Museum.)

This group may have been the staff and occupants of a children's home, around the turn of the century. (Eureka Springs Historical Museum.)

These two nurses worked at the Huntington Hospital in 1922. (Eureka Springs Historical Museum.)

A shopping spree netted the latest in fashion for these two. (Eureka Springs Historical Museum.)

The rear window of the car was a great frame for this picture. (Eureka Springs Historical Museum.)

Charles Kolb invented his water boy to help in his garden. (Eureka Springs Historical Museum.)

This saucy young woman was enjoying her vacation in Eureka Springs. (Eureka Springs Historical Museum.)

The Day family posed for their picture at their home in 1884. (Bank of Eureka Springs.)

In the photographer's studio, two girls can be recorded sitting on the moon. (Eureka Springs Historical Museum.)

Claude Fuller was prominent as an attorney, a member of the Arkansas House of Representatives, and mayor of Eureka Springs. His children are shown in front of the house and the girl on the left is driving a Packard. (Bank of Eureka Springs.)

Mary Pike, wife of the chief of police, is pictured about 1910. (Bank of Eureka Springs.)

Perhaps Edna Bergdorf had this little photograph made for a suitor. She came from a family that owned a grocery store they established in 1885. (Bank of Eureka Springs.)

Two girls sit dreamily in a window seat and contemplate the future, as most youth do at some time in their early life. (Eureka Springs Historical Museum.)

110

Tiny waists and billowy blouses were fashionable in the late 1800s. It is hard to imagine how the women coped with the warm clothing in the summer's heat. (Eureka Springs Historical Museum.)

Born in 1892, Cora Pinkley-Call spent her entire life in Carroll County, Arkansas. A writer, she produced books, short stories, and biographies and became an authority on local folklore and a naturalist. She is largely responsible for the body of knowledge that remains on Eureka Springs' history. (Eureka Springs Historical Museum.)

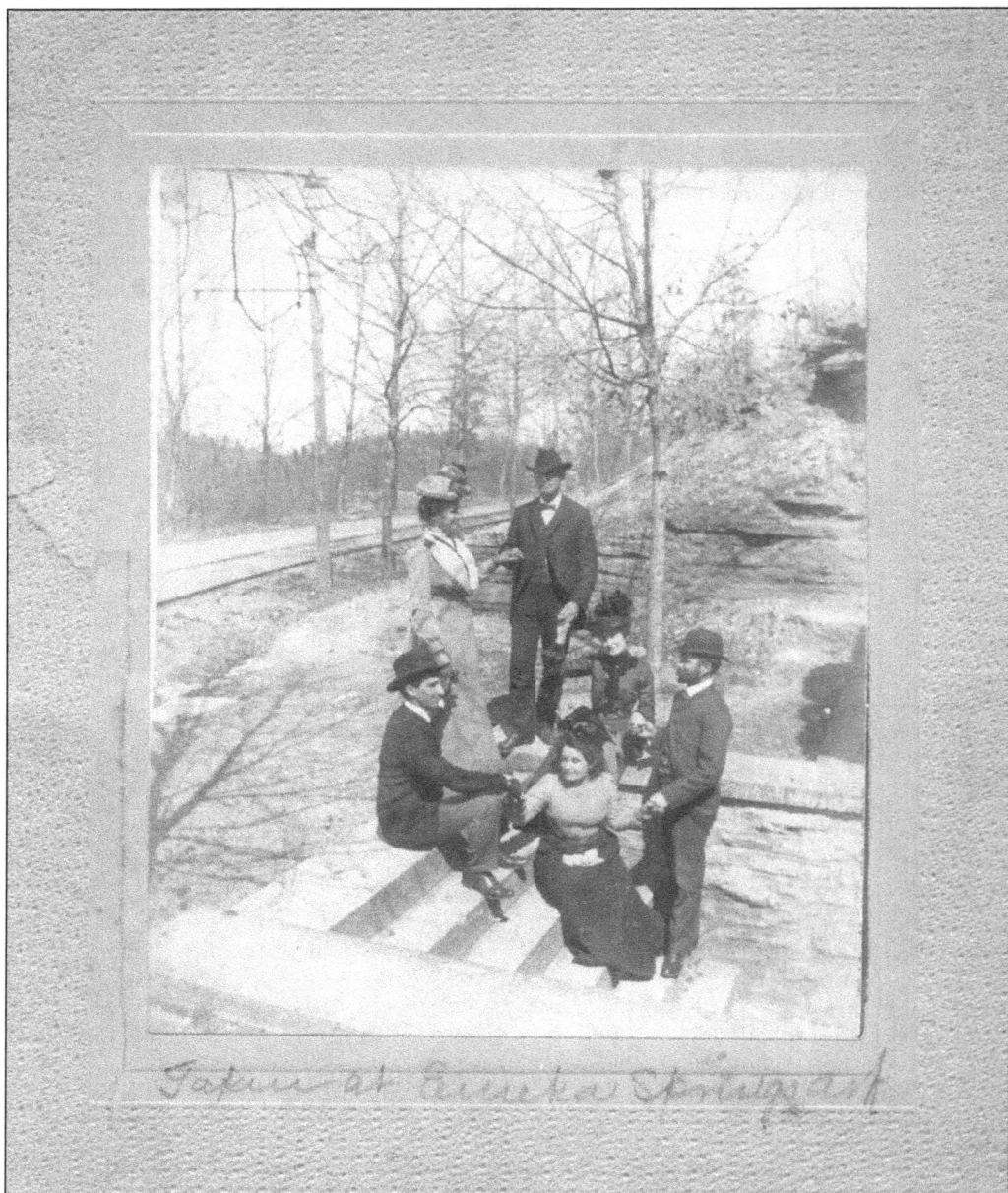

Three couples stop for a moment of reflection or prayer as they clasp hands and form a circle during their vacation activities. (Eureka Springs Historical Museum.)

Eight

ACTIVITIES

The clear mountain air, vast forests, waterways, and a beautiful, rugged landscape offered endless activities for visitor and native alike. While technology is a big part of life now, entertainment is not so different than it was 100 years ago.

Picnics are always a good choice for a day in the woods. These people found a friendly spot beside the river. (Eureka Springs Historical Museum.)

Spear fishing on the lakes and rivers required skill—not to mention the ability to stand up in the boat. (Eureka Springs Historical Museum.)

For some, the river was sport, for others it was a way of life. (Eureka Springs Historical Museum.)

A cyclist had to be pretty fit to master the ups and downs of the mountains but these two seem up to the task. (Eureka Springs Historical Museum.)

Boxing matches were popular with the men—although there are a few women and children in the crowd. The rug in the ring seems an unusual touch. (Eureka Springs Historical Museum.)

These girls may be playing May Queen, preparing for the future years. A few of the girls couldn't stand still long enough for the slow shutter speed required for the films of the 1930s and left blurs on the image. (Eureka Springs Historical Museum.)

The young women wait to begin the May Pole dance. (Eureka Springs Historical Museum.)

Lake Lucerne was a favorite gathering place for boating and swimming. (Eureka Springs Historical Museum.)

Swimming at Lake Lucerne was always an anticipated event. (Eureka Springs Historical Museum.)

These girls seem to be having a great time, although it is doubtful the donkey appreciated the assignment. (Eureka Springs Historical Museum.)

Local photographers often kept animals to use in their work. This donkey appeared in many of the pictures taken in Eureka Springs. (Eureka Springs Historical Museum.)

This animal managed to accommodate six children on its back. (Eureka Springs Historical Museum.)

There are a few different versions of this image titled *Happy at Harding Spring*. (Randy Wolfinbarger.)

Parades were a familiar form of entertainment around the turn of the century, and the whole town usually turned out for the occasion. (Bank of Eureka Springs.)

Locals would travel miles to another town for a celebration or holiday. This gathering took place in Berryville, 12-miles east of Eureka Springs. (Eureka Springs Historical Museum.)

Taking a meal could be an everyday affair or a very special occasion. (Eureka Springs Historical Museum.)

Picnics were still a popular pastime in the 1930s. (Eureka Springs Historical Museum.)

It is doubtful these people went very far in this carriage without the horse to pull it. (Eureka Springs Historical Museum.)

A picnic in the woods always worked well and the auto was right there when the ants showed up. (Eureka Springs Historical Museum.)

This horn quartette may have been in town for a convention or they might have been part of a local orchestra. No matter, they made good music. (Bank of Eureka Springs.)

The summer auditorium in Harmon Park seated 3,500 and was the site for entertainment of all kinds. However, because of fire danger, the facility had no smoking signs posted long before today's health concerns. (Bank of Eureka Springs.)

The Crescent dining room was sometimes used as a moving-picture theater. (Bank of Eureka Springs.)

More typically, the dining room was exactly that, a dining room. The space looks much as it did when it was built and is currently open as a restaurant. (Bank of Eureka Springs.)

Always considered a hunting paradise, game was plentiful for these sportsmen during the 1930s. (Randy Wolfinbarger.)

Once, large herds of elk were raised at Elk Ranch and drew hunters from all over the country. (Randy Wolfinbarger.)

125

Like 78-year-old J.D. Crawford pictured here, many local people depended on game to provide meat for their families. (Eureka Springs Historical Museum.)

Women were among the people who enjoyed fishing and this one did pretty well this day. (Eureka Springs Historical Museum.)

Bobcats were among the native wildlife hunted and taken in the Ozarks. They are still around but have declined in numbers. (Randy Wolfinbarger.)

A Native Hunter, Eureka Springs, Ark.

These men got a good catch for their day's effort in the 1940s. (Eureka Springs Historical Museum.)

127

Golfing was a popular sport for both visitors and locals, early in the century. The landscape proved to be challenge when the course was under construction, but made for a terrific game when finished. (Bank of Eureka Springs.)

Cora Pinkley-Call interviewed some of the town's old timers, Lewis Harp, Levi Howerton, C. Burton Saunders, and L. Jackson before a parade. (Bank of Eureka Springs.)